THE PHILOCALIST

the philocalist

EMILY SHEA

DAES Industries

Copyright © 2024 by Emily Shea

All rights reserved. No part of this book may be reproduced in any manner whatsoever without written permission except in the case of brief quotations embodied in critical articles and reviews.

The moral rights of the author have been asserted.

Instagram: e.s.words

Cover illustration purchased for use: https://creativemarket.com/anmark

First Printing, 2024

Contents

Dedication   x

everyday   1

the philocalist   2

a rainy day   4

childhood   6

as a child   7

beautiful   8

my child   9

God's children   10

butter sandwich   12

brothers   13

first born   14

teen son   15

night storm   16

midnight storm   17

small things	18
mum life	20
messy bun	21
miscarriage	22
one weekend	23
a poem for mothers in church	24
go to sleep	26
I don't care	28
inner voice	30
the joy of being woman	32
study	34
midnight ablutions	35
familiar	36
midnight words	37
he sleeps	38
thunder	39
sky eyes	40
wonder	41
movie night	42
darwin	43
dear... me	44

Contents ~ vii

second last day of school	46
library door	47
disappointment	48
alone	49
f words	50
matthew	51
my life a library	52
imagination	56
screen	57
cabin fever	58
unfolding	60
slow down	61
pause	62
goodnight	64
which side?	65
basketball dad	66
gelato	67
afternoon nap	68
hot water	69
toddler on a plane	70
music's embrace	71

man on the plane	72
the old man	74
lady in green	75
mumma	76
between it all	77
Grandpa	78
christmas eve	80
hope	81
Immanuel	82
by the water	83
year nine	84
home	86
another world	87
second love	88
undone	90
grey	91
just words	92
sad	94
whisky	95
old men walking dogs	96
golfer	97

waiting	98
weed	99
she will dance	100
the pilbara	101
worship	102
the liminal poet	104
the mind of a poet	106
me again	108
About The Author	110

for the philocalists...
may you continue to see beauty

everyday

somewhere in this day to day sameness
wandering through known steps
are small pieces of magic
insurmountable moments of beauty
maybe a touch
a glance
i love you
we walk these paths together
hard at times
but somehow our ebb and flow work

the philocalist

she wakes up
buries face in pillow
fart escapes cheeks
curling her body
to foetal position
then stretch
long
languid
brushing foot against his
she rolls toward
bed edge
eyes refusing
to acknowledge
morning sun

still
sleep evades her
she knows
day longingly calls her
her world
an exploration of words
to eloquently
paint the everyday
mundane in beautiful ways
that you might drink in
every moment of your
beautiful life

a rainy day

a rainy day is a day for poets
for swimming in salty water
for wrestling with sons
for looking into grey skies
and knowing words sit
waiting to fall on you

a rainy day is a day for poets
for floating as rain falls on you
for listening as it waxes and wanes
for pouring a glass of red
and writing more than one poem
because words fall everywhere

a rainy day is a day for poets
for dancing in the rain
for melancholy and murmurings
for no bra and loose shirts
and letting tears fall
to mirror the sky

a rainy day is a day for poets
for soaking children
for lost children - or maybe not so lost
for adventure and imagination
and driving endlessly
until lost children are found

a rainy day is a day for poets
for long hugs
for i love yous
for wishing life could slow down
and wondering how you survived the last year
disillusioned with where you are now

a rainy day is a day for poets
for cool winds
for palm leaves against grey skies
for laughter
and knowing words sit
waiting to fall on you

childhood

peace
you are all gone
bubbling laughter silenced
jarring voices calmed
quiet
humming fans
simmering food
stacking dishes
sigh
soon your aching tummies
will bring you home
bustling through the door
noise
and love
returns
once more

as a child

as a child accepts another
may our hearts ever love
as a child risks and tries and grows
may we step bravely forward
as a child has faith that the sun will rise tomorrow
as surely as it sets tonight
may we have faith our failures
mean the chance for rebirth
as a child sees possibilities
may barriers fall from our eyes
as a child asks a million questions
may we curiously approach the world
as a child expresses ardent love
may we learn to freely express our love

beautiful

You're beautiful.

Words breathed at the end of a sentence,
as he straightens his tall, secure frame from the crouch
he assumed so he could touch your shoulder and look into
your eyes.

Just two words.

my child

you are loved
more than you know
than you see
knees worn
hands calloused
voice softened
for my love
encompasses you
from the moment
conceived and hidden
grown and revealed
held and kissed
leaned on and held up
you are always
extravagantly loved
for you will always
be my child

God's children

i think
i understand
a little of how God feels
His children
living with small regard
for humankind
watching my own children
intentionally hurt
breaking my heart
that peaceful natures
are not more prevalent
for once a child
is tethered to your heart
they reflect you
but also their own nature
which is broken
as is mine
and i cannot expect perfection
when my own darkness
robs moments of peace

despite this
i love them fiercely
as my Father loves me
and i would move mountains
split oceans
traverse valleys
to see them come home
find solace
renew hope
as He does for me

butter sandwich

the sweetest gifting
butter sandwich by mr eight
soothing mum's tears

brothers

my blood
my brother
distance
does not distil
my love
nor time
though I
may not
see you
each day
our hearts
are banded
through dirt and dust
joy and tears
work and love
and much laughter
we are two
but one
from the same
bright sun
and always
will be

first born

moments like this
scratch my back mum
before you sleep
hugs every time
you pass me
I love you
called out as you leave
whispered in my ear
said while wrapping
your arms around my neck
then releasing your weight
all these
outweigh the angst
the tired and grumpy
the teen brain
none come close
in my memory
to your sweetness
I love you

teen son

sweetness overflows
as hand-hearts made and lips speak
love you through window

night storm

cracking sky
wakes slumbering humans
rumbles and rain
its offering today

midnight storm

midnight blackness
dark grey clouds
hide all light
sharp rain patters
here then gone
on sleeping house
I alone awake
listening to child's
gentle breath
warmth escaping
their nostrils
as patters return
drowning all sound

small things

the hard times
when you walk through them
take time to notice small things
a sparkle in a stranger's eye
ice cream on a child's face
a new flavour on your tongue
the remedy of laughter
anything shared
a smile
a joke
a touch
a kiss
a sigh
a story
a breath
a heartbeat in sync
passionate conversation
multiple glasses of wine
a steadying hand on your back
freshly brewed coffee
a familiar face
restful sleep

a clean floor
in these you will see
a small glimpse of grace
in these you will feel
a small sense of wholeness
and the healing from hard will
begin in the small things

mum life

I go to shower
I need a towel
I walk the hallway
linen cupboard beckoning
I stop to put the washing on
I put a book away
I get a drink of water
little ones call my name
they fall asleep
I go to shower
I need a towel

messy bun

messy bun
her underwear clad body
wrapped in flannelette
as academic writing
floods her screen
eyes full of edits
ears full of mum
cat jokes, lizard jokes
where's my...
checking newly pierced ears
have you...
eat breakfast
get dressed
shoes on
I'm gonna ride today mum
lukewarm coffee
patiently waiting
for the next sip
child across lap
as writing fades to black
and energy is spent elsewhere

miscarriage

you were a moment
unexpected
life-changing
only known a handful of weeks
only held in my womb
a piece of my heart in heaven

one weekend

birth . engagement . cancer
in one weekend
three . lives . changed
many hearts impacted
hope . lies . here

a poem for mothers in church

a sigh as you see another person stare towards your children
they are silent but their hands create from plastic blocks in imitation of their creator God
the music swells and their mouths join the chorus as their hands create
you sit to tousle their hair and remind them of God's love as communion comes around and they give thanks replacing their creations with bread and juice
one by one people speak and they pick up the creations again making angels with wings and power to protect them as we talked about at home
as they go to fellowship with their peers your mother heart relaxes and you find your place in worship
you quietly scoop the plastic blocks away and allow the words to tend to your weary soul
you have been the only source of life for these children for a week

every question is yours to answer
every fight yours to referee
every hurt yours to soothe
every tear yours to wipe
every wrong yours to right
so if you see this mother with plastic blocks around her feet
rejoice that she has made it through the week
rejoice that she has brought her children into fellowship
in a place where she feels loved and supported and not judged
rejoice that she can still smile and sing
and wonder at why you stare

go to sleep

I lie
feet next to your head
breathing slowly
thunder rolls
you cough
roll over
my foot is dead
so I roll it
grimacing in the dark
it's after ten
I think
my abs twitch
I question
how long
do eight year olds
take to fall asleep...
after having a two hour
afternoon sleep
sigh
it appears
a while

...

especially after
hijacking
their brothers bed
talking til mum got home
talking while mum had a shower
laughing through bedroom walls
...
sleep can I have it yet?
eleven year old above me
scratching at something
scratch
high-pitched scratch
my brain
ugh
stop
please sleep
I want to sleep
but not upside down
on your bed
...
a-choo
your large sleepy sneeze
and short snuffles
my eyes
so tired
as I fight
to stay awake

I don't care

"I don't care"

It slipped out of my lips again, as my almost 8 year old yelled about the niggling comment his brother made.
My heart sank, as I played the rhetoric that harries every mother's mind when they make a parenting mistake. How can you not care about this moment in your child's life? How could you say that to this child you love? You're a terrible mother.

Truth is, I have spent my day listening to the heartaches of others, as their weariness is showing in this end of term.

Truth is, I have held space for a colleague who is struggling with difficult students.

Truth is, I have carried a burden of worry over my oldest child's education support, and what I could do to make it better.

Truth is, I didn't complete my own work today in order to cover classes of sick teachers, and I know I must complete this once my kids are asleep.

Truth is, I care very much that my children are not giving each other the compassion I also long to give them, but maybe we are all just at our wits end.

So today I give compassion to myself, to fail forward in this parenting journey, and to take back my 'I don't care', and replace it with a long hug and whispered love.

inner voice

a small
patient moment
step by shuffling step
I will grow compassionately
lending myself kindness
so often shown
to others

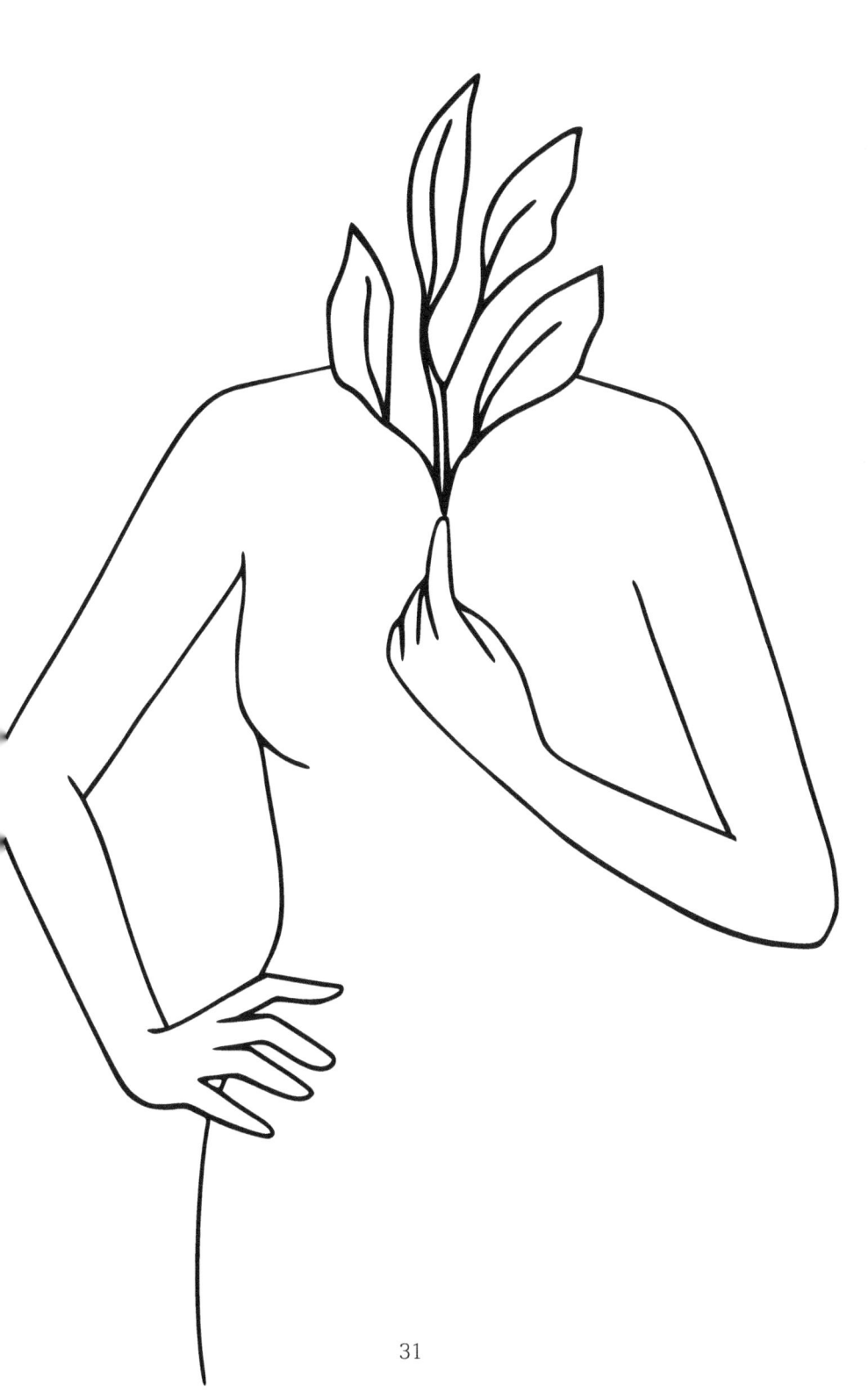

the joy of being woman

sometimes I forget
the joy of being woman
and demote myself to body
bloated and blimp-like
luteal phase
hungry for carbs
and slow at the gym
forgetting how strong I felt
two weeks ago
ovulating and alive
slim and strong
so strong
I was fun too
dancing in my kitchen
full of energy
I forget a woman is all seasons
in one month

we wax and wane
as the moon
it is no wonder
that we are mystery and motion
that we are life and lethargy
we create and rest and shed and rise
so cyclical
aligned with nature
the joy of being woman

study

surrounded by paper
academic words
flood the screen
uncomfortable shirt
and pants
hang over
a nearby lounge
grey blanket
smooshed between
cheeks and chair
for comfort
as tired eyes
and yawning mouth
protest the rigour
and forced participation
of late night
writing

midnight ablutions

she wakes
her midnight body
gently aching
she wrestles
to relieve herself
or roll back
the sweet oblivion
sleep beckons her
she rises
eyes shut
feet sure
her body relieved
she seeks
the warmth of bed
again

familiar

you are hard to write for
your familiar frame
rising and falling
next to me
patterns the same
known for so long
security
safety
your offering to me
despite this
your absence is long
my heart is dry
your return offers
little refreshing
dry I remain

midnight words

you groan
mumbling something
about backs
and room
rolling over
reaching for
my hip
whistle breath
settling back
into rhythm

he sleeps

that annoying sound
your husband's deep sleep breathing
while sleep eludes you

thunder

his fart shook the bed
as wet season storms thundered
in skies above
his breathing turned to heavy snores
as deafening rain joined the chorus of noise
disrupting my sleep

sky eyes

the sky is in your eyes
but you do not know it
palest blue
I don't look as often
maybe I should
these eyes hold laughter
tears and fire
they light up
catching mine

wonder

it's been too long
since I looked
longingly, longly
into your sky eyes
not stopping
to wonder
about your becoming
or curiously considering
you
I am becoming more
spreading aching wings
turning
to fly into
the sky
but the sky
is in your eyes

movie night

bodies draped
over couch cushions
legs layered
hands clasped
monday night movie
with you

darwin

my feet have planted themselves
deep here
despite thinking our time would be short
years have flowed on
children have grown
this has become home
love and heartache
joy and misery
nothing is new under the sun
this is true
of me and you
finding hope in dark places
uprooting feet
we will move on one day
taking love with us

dear... me

dear seventeen
I wish I had been bolder for you
followed my instinct
pursued travel
known options existed
outside my bubble

dear eighteen
I wish you'd been brave enough to make the call yourself
that others' opinions
didn't matter as much
as your opinion of yourself
you worked so hard
so hard
and caught up
on what you thought
was failure to know what you wanted

dear nineteen
God works for good for those who love him
he does
he did
he still will
even when you can't hear his voice for the noise

dear thirty nine
some days it feels like you are that unsure teen again
but remember
you are bolder
you trust yourself
you are strong and courageous
you still work hard
you have achieved more than you could have imagined
God still works
you are a lioness
raising a generation
you are capable
he will equip you

second last day of school

drown me now
exhaustion
tipping sanity
into tired yawns
unsteady feet
head in hands
gin in glass
dinner cooking
due dates hanging
brain mush
one more day
the catch cry
survive
just one
more
day

library door

the kind of day
you lean
against the slow
closing door
resistance felt
its pressure
gently moving you
staring blankly
face passive
clunking into place
you move again

disappointment

if I've learnt anything
it's that disappointment does not discriminate
it touches each heart
it comes when you expect it
and when you least expect it
I'm not sure which is worse
I've learnt that holding anything tight
is a sure way to meet disappointment
but to have no expectations
seems like a settling life
and I don't want to settle
I want to soar
even if arrows of disappointment
catch my heels
and drag me down
I can pull them out
heal
and soar again
why should disappointment dictate
I am the master of my responses
and I choose to soar
with joy

alone

waiting
it's a time of stillness
isn't it?
life could be churning around me
but I am alone
and still
I don't know anyone here
in this space
no familiarity
just me
and who I am here
I'm not important to anyone
no one here needs me
relies on me
for they do not know me
my humanity connects me
but I feel alone
I wonder
do others sit alone in crowds
feeling alone

f words

fierce tears
frustration and forgiveness
fraught feelings
finding finality
in failing feet

matthew

you are missed
in locked eyes and broad smiles over an inside joke
at family birthdays as nephews grow another year
in unhindered, bubbling up and overflowing laughter
in warm hugs, cold beers and hot BBQs

my life a library

the cleansing work
of taking down the books
wiping off the dust
and leafing through
the sacred memories
a twenty dollar note found on the road
mum forgetting the bus pick up
dad's bible on the table
early mornings and aftershave
ironing hankies and braiding doll's hair
fishing and prawning
backyard obstacle courses
monkey bars and cubby houses
saturday morning tv
hospital trips and brother sick
prayers and anointing
life and death
baptism of water
falling in love too many times
graduating and loving friends
making donuts
vodka and panadol and sleeping

falling in love for good
lost scarves and hands held
family moving and heart aching
rings and weddings
first homes
graduation and work
colleagues and students
new friends and old
friday night barbecues
babies
more babies
building a house
even more babies
lost memories
lost brain cells... maybe
a lost baby
30
another baby
selling a house
living with parents
moving away

far away
new things, friends, work
another lost baby
life goes on
study begins

children grow
past students' babies
a leadership role
study pauses
love wavering
teens
grief
love of old friends
faithfulness of God
love growing
soul awakening
poetry
study begins again

pause

place this book back

a new year beckons
face it with eyes open
expectant

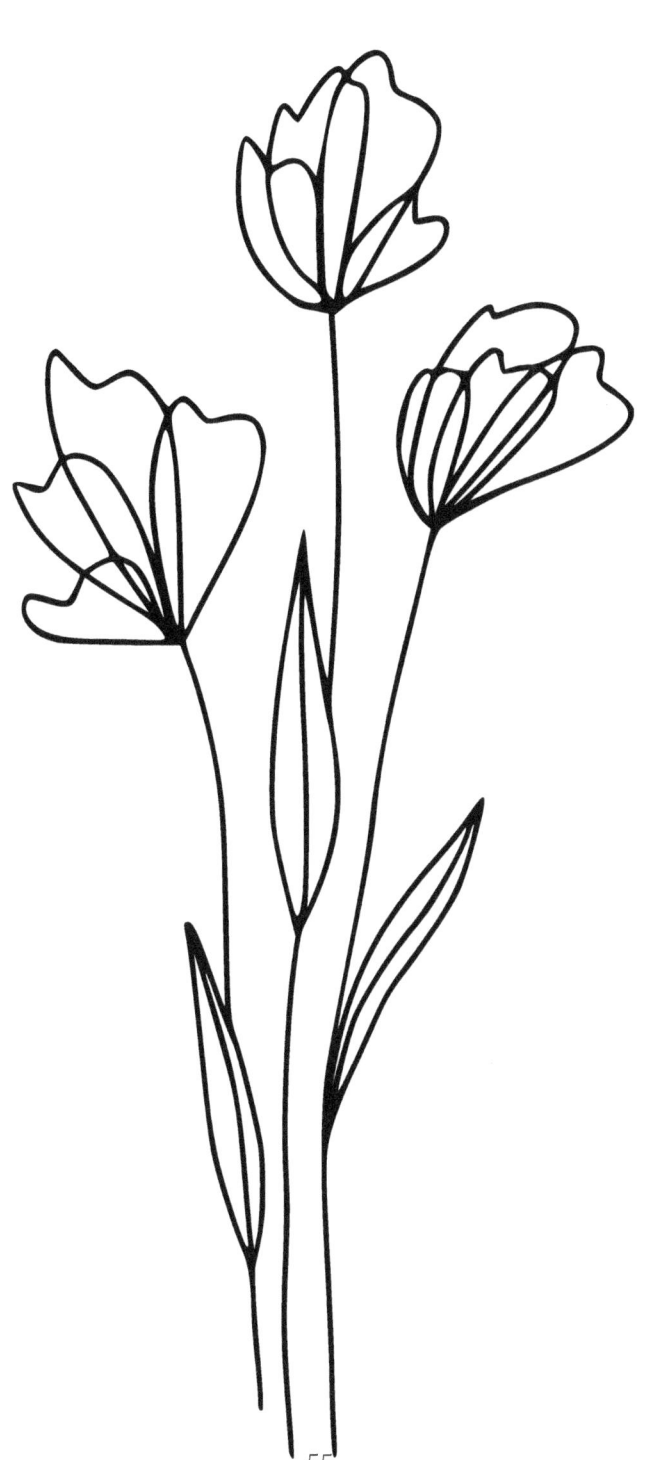

imagination

rain
i do love you
but moreso
when i am
tucked tightly
undercover
holding
bound paper
mind exploring
trails
wound by
others
worlds opening
to possibility
losing time
gaining wealth
in the rain

screen

ever-present
this tug of values
of glassy reflection
that beckons
our faces
to stare
tear my eyes
away
to be present
one with flesh
pressing hands
and lips together
catching eyes
truly seeing
the other
mirrored in iris
and heart
rather than
panes of glass

cabin fever

rain
five days
straight
monotonous skies
give this
tropical girl
sun

croaking frogs
happiest
in the wet
then plants
soaking in nourishment

grass grows
and grows
and grows
no fear of mower
or blade
to stifle it
thrashing trees
superseded
by quiet drips
as wind dies
moments pass

stillness

sudden rain
beats all
into submission
traps us inside
again

unfolding

spontaneous
you embrace life
fascinated by
small things
entrepreneur
you seize opportunities
I wait at home
small boys my company
little hearts to nurture
as you age
you slow
preferring home
comfortable with how things are
my boys have grown
feel my wings unfold
the sky now mine

slow down

sometimes
it is good
to travel behind the bin truck
to feel those pangs
of hurry
and remind
them
it is ok
to drive slowly
that a few kilometres
at a slower pace
is ok

pause

pause
in evening
in storms
in laundry
in raised voices
in g&t
in dinner cooking
in child raising
in bandaid placement
in consoling
in solitude
among people
in attempted grace
in late work
in food ordering

in phone calls
in listening
in teaching
in head aching
in forgetting
in devotion
in smiling
in sighing
in frowning
in coffee
in morning
wake

goodnight

goodnight
from a stranger
who shared a laugh
when you forgot
where you parked your car

which side?

a shared laugh
dancing the steps
pondering which side
to cross paths

basketball dad

dear basketball dad
i see you
carrying your daughter on your ribs
kissing her little cheek
walking towards the bubblers
water bottle of another child
in the other hand
you speak volumes
in your simple acts
of kindness

gelato

a knowing glance
between mums
as she says
"you can't complain
of a sore tummy
and not eat lunch
and then want two scoops
of gelato"
I smile
my children with their dad
knowing this is me
has been me
will be me again
so I laugh
and write this down

afternoon nap

sublime moment
head meets pillow
rain thunders
on tin roof
afternoon nap
perfection

hot water

the water ran hot
slowly
dissolving ochre sauce
remnants of dinner
spent with love
dark
the window before me
reflecting light
above
papers on bench
wafting in fan wind
I see reflection
peripheral
haphazard movement
water runs over
my writing stops

toddler on a plane

the uncontrollable laughter
of a toddler
on a plane
my heart smiles

music's embrace

you wrap me in music
longing hits my chest
dinner prep forgotten
as eyes spill over

man on the plane

the intimate bumping of elbows
as 5'2 and 6'3
adjust seatbelts
soft skin noticing the other
then pulling away
to allocated space
sleep capturing eyes
elbow bumps thigh
quickly
no lingering
jolted awake
adjusting again
head resting against too hard window
eyes closed
chin on hand
head slowly slipping forward
bump
awake
head jolts
sigh

sleep hard to come by here
movement slow
stay in own space
but I need to pee
up
out
walk the aisle
the hum follows
one up
two up
sliding back in
seatbelt on
intimate elbows
bump soft skin
again

the old man

weathered
and aged
my step
falters
as I follow
young legs
running
full of life
joy and hope

weathered
and aged
I shuffle behind
my eyes
still spark
adventure
stretching before you
and I
along for the ride

lady in green

she leaned her wrinkled face closer
face mirrored in equally weathered skin
and in this moment solidarity
aged women
sparkling eyes
seeing lifetimes
I would never know
passing each other
leaning on trolleys for stability
"you're well put together today"
"pardon?"
noisy shopping centre
impacting this communication
"your outfit is lovely... you look beautiful"
radiant
beaming
"thank you"

mumma

mumma
when did you age
your jet black hair
gently softening to grey
you are still strong
the weight of life and love
carried in your heart
mumma
i see your smile
i know but a piece
of the joy and heartache
lying underneath
the sweetness of one
who knows grief
mumma
i honour you
who loved unconditionally
who led little children
holding hands and hearts
your wisdom golden
faithful and steadfast

between it all

I hope you know
the words
between it all
music shared
clothes washed
hugs given
poetic reminders
tears shed
lunch made
couch snuggles
everyday reminders
long embraces
have you got...
all the things
I love you

Grandpa

I slept under Scorpio last night
it reminded me of you
your already worn hands
unlatching gates
guiding grandkids along dark paths
as early morning stars
looked down on us
you named them then
pointing our faces skyward
showing Scorpio swirl
Orion's belt
the big dipper
4am memories

waiting for cows to come
calling them in
they knew your voice
we followed your every footstep
secure that grandpa knew each one
he walked familiar trails
leading us to the dairy
teaching us to clean an udder
shovel manure
scooping fresh milk from the vat
with cream on top
Scorpio looked down upon me then
and does again

christmas eve

christmas eve
beach walks are
for kite surfers
for metal detectors
for rubbish collectors
and dog walkers
for nudists
for families
for mothers and daughters
and friends
for broken shells and urchins
and crabs and sticks
for driftwood and barnacles
for trudging through wet sand
for salty winds
for storms
dirty water
and incoming tides

hope

threads of hope
weaving wispy strands
despite written words
threatening to end plans
half-made
waited for
let the tears fall
if they must
we were made to feel
let the helplessness
wash over you
as the uncertain world spins
carrying you
in its cycle
where men and women
make plans
and try to save the world
remember another's uncertainty
as she held God in her arms
a tiny baby
our only hope

Immanuel

Immanuel
to grief and shame
to tears and ash
to dirt and mire
to heartache
to misconception
to frailty and failure
to sorrow and death
to chaos and despair
Immanuel
to sweetness and hope
to joy and laughter
to kindness and grace
to healing and wholeness
to freedom
to life and light
to new beginnings
to peace and truth
Immanuel

by the water

eyes shut
eolian whispers
caress cheeks
brilling seagulls
curlew wail
echoing back
laughing children
water splashing
ocean swimming
peaceful afternoon

year nine

fourteen.fifteen
it's a journey you know
sometimes we slip
off the stepping stone
or we jump and miss
expectations are high
so we swim to the next
climb on
and try again
we might not make it every time
but we have the confidence to try again
we've been given support
and shown we have courage
and purpose
we can leave behind baggage
and friendships

we can speak up
we can be strong in our words
if shaken
our friends lend their arms
their shoulders
their warmth
until our feet are steady
and firm again
we may not be ok
straight away
or ever
life has thrown a lot our way
but we are still strong
we learn
we grow
fourteen.fifteen
it's a journey you know

home

you are home to me
no matter what age
coming back to you
will always be
coming home
for we hold
each others hearts
tenderly and gently
knowing the value
in being loved
with compassion
and understanding

another world

if hands
could reach
through screens
I'd flow
full bodied
to you
hand gently
cupping face
eyes gazing
arms enveloping
being enveloped
joyful tears
spilling relief
relaxing bodies
finally home

second love

for Ant, Lis, & Lauren

I think
I've learnt
watching you
life is so short
nothing is permanent
but love can happen
more than once
and that grief
is a beautiful mess
of emotions
that never leaves us
second chances happen
and hearts can
hold infinite love
more love
than we could imagine

when we first find love
our heart is full
or so we think
children expand it
friends expand it
lost love breaks it
sometimes
second love fills it
love is abundant
this is
what I've learnt

undone

and all I wanted
was to wrap it all up
and push it away
instead I got curious
and teased it out
tight knots turning into
frayed edges
grasping for strands
I see it clearer now
the knot untied
I am not hard
I am soft
I am undone
and that is beautiful

grey

blankness
uncertainty
I can't even write
except this
short
pathetic excuse
for a poem
because
I feel everything
and nothing
I see greys
bleary eyed
but
pink leaves
highlight
my grey sky
so it leaves me
unsure
but certain
that beauty
still exists
when I am grey

just words

that's just it
I guess
just words
I have
no fancy
metaphors
today
just words
but each
I place
just so
inflection
here
so you know
I love you
I miss you
I can't abide you

I don't think
words always
must paint
images
sometimes
they are
just words
and we use them
because
they are familiar
necessary
simple
sometimes
just words
are ok

sad

red wine and sadness
brimming tears ruin the view
lashes close tear drops

whisky

water of life
you are heat
and smoke
fire and burn
on my tongue
slipping down
warming hearts

old men walking dogs

to the two older men walking their dogs this afternoon

the first, stepping aside and telling his dog
"say hello to everyone"
pulled me out of melancholy with a wave, a "hello" and
a laugh

the second, clipping the lead on
and commenting "he's an asshole sometimes"
as you passed me
followed by "come on son" as I walked on
brought a laugh to my eyes

your kindness is appreciated

golfer

the lone
man in black
shouldered his caddy bag
sunset clouds
softening sky
behind him
twice I saw him
rounding different bends
peaceful
focussed
him and the green
and his thoughts

waiting

waiting
the after school traffic
lines up
air heavy
wet grass smells
fill nostrils
check the bench
slightly damp I sit anyway
sky mirrored
in puddles
other worlds to explore
I wonder if you can fall through?
the calm after the storm
the calm before the storm
bell rings
they flood out
small bodies rushing
not unlike the storm
to the gates
my job
to hold back the rush
with a single gate

weed

can beauty not come from brevity
the pared back
flung open door to
unfurled space

air

golden fields
wide expansive skies
a simple five petalled white flower
bursting from a fluffy weed

she will dance

patterns of culture
her body moving
to the unheard
music
chant maybe
floating in the humid air
feet tapping concrete
shopping bags
beside her
yet
connection
she feels it
tangible
in thick air
in unheard rhythms
in ancient culture
and so
she will dance

the pilbara

your strong, passionate voice
carried across the humid air
I turned to see you
bald head
white beard
sitting in wheelchair
with one leg
your mate laughing as you recall
stories of adventure
"you go above the 26th parallel
it's the best country in the world
the Pilbara"
interest peaked
I had to know
what your words meant
I wanted to make sure
you were remembered
in my words
your passion
everyday joviality
made me smile
in the darkness

worship

there are rhythms here
of wind in leaves
in cycles of seasons
rhythms in swirl of dried riverbed
sand shifting with each visit
footsteps rhythmic on red ground
sandy ground, rocky ground
rhythms in still water
silent
in fish plops
and shimmering sun
greater rhythms in sun rising
sun setting
and moon orbits
brightest in night skies
comforting great rhythms
meaning tomorrow is new and starts again
for you
it's shifting
if you listen
sit in silence in shade of gorge
she sings to you in windy whispers

creation moves in unseen rhythms
set in motion by creator
who doesn't need these rhythms
for he does not slumber or sleep
who causes the sun to rise on you
and brings life
he is outside it all
yet in it all
to the tiniest ant
his rhythms visible
they know his voice
as he calls the winds from their corners
spirit whispers in wind around me
walking ancient pathways
nestled in valleys
traversing mountains
today this is my worship

the liminal poet

the poet sat
back against the doorframe
of bedroom and ensuite
tv sounds float through
her door
halfway between
post-walk sweat
still shod
contemplating a shower
needing to write
thoughts from the walk
sights
of golfer
dogs
dusky clouds over water
more hellos than usual
sunset over green golf hills

natures glory
trees bowing
wind caressing
water engulfing
fully immersed in moments
words forming
describing
capturing memory
and moment
on a page

the mind of a poet

a blessing or curse
the mind of a poet
all moments captured
in words on a page
joy bubbling
spilling over
expressing elation
laugh escapes
grief tearing
soul and sinew
gasping air
between sobs
passionate embrace
souls entwined
soft skin
lithe bodies

memories of a friend
who lived there once
need to connect again
digress
she thinks
long yawn
stifling coherent thought
clutter calling her to rise
to finish jobs
all she wants
is sleep

me again

and I wasn't sure what I wanted anymore
but it did seem to find itself
in writing so some of life made sense
and floating in salty ocean waves
procuring memories from time
and closing eyes to see you dance
in childhood arms flung around waists
and taking time to breathe...
just breathe
and here I am being me
again

Emily is a Jesus follower, a wife, a mother to four boys, an educator, a musician, a curious and thoughtful soul.

She has written songs from her teenage years and poetry from time to time.

More recently, her poetic work has flowed out of life, relationships and all the complexities of loving and being loved.

These poems also find home in her love for nature, hiking, climbing, and the healing gift of swimming in the ocean. Seeing beauty in everyday moments as a way to celebrate the life we live.

This is her second collection of poetry.